Anne-Katrin Hagen

From Flatwork to Jumping

Schooling over Poles

Contents

Imprint

Copyright of original edition © 2004 by Cadmos Verlag
GmbH, Brunsbek
Copyright of English edition © 2004 by Cadmos Verlag
GmbH, Brunsbek
Translated by: Claire Williams
Project management: Editmaster Co Ltd, Northampton
Design and setting: Ravenstein, Verden.
Photography: Chr. Krumm, Andreas Blast
Cover Photos: Chr. Krumm
Illustrations: Ester von Hacht
Printed by Westermann Druck, Zwickau.
All rights reserved
Copying or storage in electronic media is
permitted only with the prior written permission
of the publishers.
Printed in Germany

ISBN 3-86127-947-9

A rider needs a balanced seat and must be able to use her hands independently from the movement of the horse.

Why school over poles?

Schooling over poles is important for horses, whether the horse is going to be used for dressage, eventing or show jumping. Working over poles exercises the horse and strengthens its muscles, especially those of the back. It encourages suppleness and elasticity and will help to improve the horse's rhythm. Work over cavalletti is also a good preparation for show jumping. Working over varied low jumping grids will help to secure a rider's seat as well as develop a better feeling for the rhythm in canter and through a grid. It also helps a rider to learn to judge distances to and between jumps.

Working over cavalletti and poles is enjoyable for both horse and rider. It brings variety to everyday training, especially in wintertime when it is not always possible to hack out as often.

How well do you need to ride?

Anyone who can hack out confidently, is not scared of a brisk canter and does not grip with their legs or hang onto the reins should have few problems starting to school over poles.

Hacking out is the easiest way to learn how your horse is going to react to the unknown. You have to expect the unexpected, so a sudden shy or a small pop over tree roots won't unseat you. However you should only start jumping when you have developed an independent seat.

This means that you are able to use all of the aids independently of the others. You must have a balanced seat and be able to use the aids through the reins without being affected by the movement of the horse.

What type of horse is suitable?

If you have never jumped at all then it is best to use an experienced, well-trained horse that jumps willingly and safely when starting out. But even a horse that knows its job should be ridden regularly by a more experienced rider, to keep up its level of training and to stop it getting stale. Even the safest of jumpers will easily lose confidence if he doesn't get the right information from his rider before and after the jump. If a learner bumps back down on his back, or hangs onto his mouth over the jump if he jumps too big because the stride was off, or if he hurts himself by hitting a rail, it is all too easy for a reliable jumper to turn into a frequent refuser. This shouldn't put anyone off starting to ride over small obstacles, but it is important to understand that you need to approach the enjoyment of jumping with a sense of respons- ibility. You can do more damage to your horse over jumps than by just working on the flat. Once a horse becomes "soured" it is very hard to sweeten him to jumping again.

Here both are properly equipped for jumping. The rider is wearing a hard hat, body protector, gloves and riding boots and the horse is tacked up with bridle and martingale, jumping saddle and brushing boots.

What equipment does the rider need?

A correctly fitted hard hat to the latest standard is a must. It is vital that the hat is fitted properly by a trained retailer, so that in the event of a fall it doesn't either slip backwards and hurt your neck, or tip forward and risk breaking or damaging your nose. Long fringes or a thick plait or pony tail stuffed up under the hat won't help even the most expensive hat fit properly. Long hair needs to be tied back or put in a hairnet, and fringes should be tucked up under the hat.

A body protector is also a good idea, especially for beginners. When starting to ride over small jumps, it is best to wear long boots, jodhpur boots or boots with half chaps. The soles of any footwear worn should be smooth with a small heel; avoid wearing footwear fastened with Velcro straps or laces that might get caught up. Nothing should be able to get caught up in the stirrup irons – in the event of a fall, the foot should be able to immediately slip out of the stirrup. It should go without saying that trainers or sneakers are totally unsuitable and even potentially dangerous.

How should the horse be tacked up?

In order to be able to ride correctly in a forward seat in a jumping position you will need a jumping, eventing or a forward-cut general purpose saddle. No particular type of bit is necessary; a simple snaffle as normally used should be sufficient. A martingale is only necessary for a horse that may tend to toss his head. Brushing or tendon boots or bandages should be used on the front legs. On the back legs often only, ankle boots are sufficient to avoid injury.

Tip

■ ■ ■ ■

Doing anything to increase your safety is neither a sign of fear nor bad riding. Even the most experienced of riders can and do fall off.

It is also sensible to wear gloves. Many horses get stronger over jumps compared to on the flat. Since your hands are carried closer to the horse's neck, you may find that your knuckles get rubbed against his neck. It is much better to wear gloves to avoid this, since you can't give the right aids with sore hands. Depending on a horse's nature you may also need short spurs and possibly a jumping whip. Check with your riding instructor if in any doubt.

Brushing boots on the front legs and ankle or brushing boots on the back legs will help avoid injury.

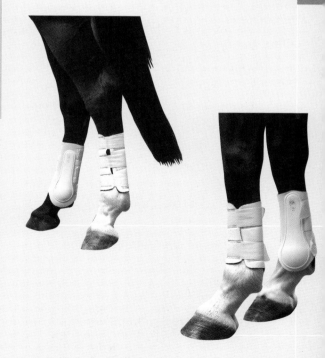

15–20 cm   30–35 cm   50 c

The most common type of cavalletti.

What are cavalletti?

In general, cavalletti are wooden poles with a wooden cross fixed at each end. The crosses are fixed on the pole so that when it is rolled, the pole will take up one of three different heights: these range from a height of 15 – 20 centimetres in the low position, to 30 – 35 centimetres in the next position, and when the pole is at its highest point it shouldn't be any higher than 50 centimetres.

The older types of cavalletti can be slightly dangerous, especially when the cross ends have sharp edges or if they are stacked one on top of another. There are many more modern variations involving loose poles that move or fall off when knocked. Alternatively the end support itself may be made of hollow plastic that is weighted down by filling it with water. It is shaped to support the poles at different heights – this type is one of the safest, as they are unlikely to cause injury if they are knocked over. If you can't get professionally built cavalletti, it is easy enough to build your own. You will need a pole (one that is sufficiently weighty) and a squared-off block of wood of the same overall

dimensions as a cavalletti cross for each end. Each block of wood then has a piece cut out of it to fit the pole onto.

You can easily build cavalletti like this yourself.

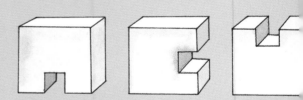

Tip

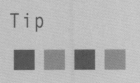

Be careful when you lay out loose poles on the ground. They are easily moved if a horse steps on or knocks them, resulting in a potentially dangerous stumble. An injury to the fetlock or tendons can result.

More lightening of the weight through the seat in the forward position.

A less obvious lighter seat.

The forward position

It is possible to differentiate between a light seat and a forward seat, depending on how much pressure is exerted down through the horse's back. In a lighter seat, the rider stays seated in the saddle but exerts less pressure, i.e. lightens through the seat, than in a dressage position. A light seat is also particularly sensible when riding young horses or when hacking out. When show jumping you should use a light seat when approaching the jumps and when riding tight turns.

In a forward seat you relieve the horse's back even more and adjust yourself to your horse's movement, the movement often being stronger than would be expected when riding on the flat. The forward seat is most easily ridden in a jumping saddle, as the wider forward-cut saddle flaps enable you to have shorter stirrups and the flatter seat gives you more room for upper body movement.

When starting out, shorten the stirrups by two to three holes. When jumping, the stirrups are usually four or five holes shorter than when riding dressage. The length will vary slightly depending on your leg length and height. Your knee will be more bent thanks to the shorter stirrups (hence the larger, forward-cut flaps) and you will find that it is easier to move your seat up and down from the saddle. In a forward position you can adapt to the horse's movement much more easily. When the horse's centre of gravity shifts when jumping, going up or down-hill, or when galloping, it is easier for you to stay balanced and exert either more or less weight through the seat as required. Any changes should be fluid and you should try to remain balanced over your own centre of gravity, regardless of how the horse is moving. In addition you need to be able to adjust to the horse's movement and constantly changing centre of gravity. None of this is as easy as it may (or may not!) sound. Standing on the ground, try keeping your balance when swaying back and forth. It goes without saying that you will need to practise your forward seat in trot and canter. Unfortunately this isn't always done in jumping lessons these days.

This is the position assumed in the forward seat.

Tip

The ball of the foot, lower leg and knee form the foundation for the rider's position in the forward seat. It is on this foundation that you can build a well balanced seat.

What is the forward position?

The widest part of the foot should rest on the stirrup treads. In a jumping saddle, your heels should be the lowest part of your body; they should not be tense but should be supple, acting as a shock absorber. They should have enough weight down through them to ensure that they stop the lower leg from slipping back. Your calves will lie against the horse's side and your knees will be bent at a greater angle thanks to the shorter stirrup length. Your knees should be laid firmly against the saddle, but without gripping, otherwise your calves are likely to lose their contact with the horse. The position of the knee (sometimes called the knee pivot point) is the critical point of the rider's posture in this forward position.

Tip

If the rider loses the pivot point through the knee, the whole position is endangered.

Even when your seat comes out of the saddle at higher speeds, you shouldn't tense up or hunch your back. You need to stay balanced! The shoulder, knee and the ball of the foot should form a vertical line.

Tip

In a forward seat, as when riding dressage, a stiff or unsteady upper body with tense or rounded shoulders or hollow back is incorrect and will interfere with the horse.

The rider here adapts her seat to the shape of the horse over the jump.

Your lower leg (not the spurs!) takes over more of the forward driving aids since your seat, which is lighter, can no longer contribute to pushing the horse on. If the lower leg slips or swings back and forth in time to the canter, you will lose your balance and this will interfere with the horse. Your upper body will, depending on the degree of lightening through the seat, be more or less bent forward from the hips. Your bottom stays, in the case of a light seat, in the saddle but exerts little if any pressure through the seat. When riding at speed or when jumping, your bottom will come out of the saddle some 10 to 20 centimetres. You should aim to stay in balance over your centre of gravity, in other words over the ball of the foot and knees – the position's foundation, with the upper body remaining supple.

Your head should be held naturally and your gaze should be directed forward through the horse's ears. Your arms should be carried in front of your body from relaxed, slightly pulled back shoulders and your hands should be held low against the horse's neck. The reins will therefore need to be shortened. Your lower arm and the reins should form a straight line to the bit. In the forward position your shoulder, knee and ball of foot form a vertical line. Your head is held slightly in front of this vertical line, while your hips, especially at higher speed, will act as a flywheel and together with the lower leg will form the driving force .

Riding on the flat, the forward position should in principle be exactly the same as when going over a jump. Because you have to adapt your centre of gravity to that of your horse, whose own centre of gravity is greatly shifted when taking off, in flight over the jump and when landing, you must adapt your own position to that of the horse's curve of flight over the jump. That may sound complicated, but actually it isn't. Most riders will do this instinctively. It is useful though to clarify how this should look and how mistakes may happen. The position can go wrong when the stirrups are too long, enabling the lower leg to slip too far back, leading to the heel being pulled up and tipping the upper body too far forward. This in turn leads to your bottom coming too far out of the saddle. When this happens, the contact to the horse's mouth usually disappears too, leaving you in front of the movement. Alternatively you will be behind the movement when your upper body is left behind, your lower legs are stretched too far forward and your hands are working backwards. In both cases a rhythmic approach to the jump will be impossible!

The rider is in front of the movement.

Here the rider is behind the movement.

This doesn't make a pretty picture!

The rider hasn't lightened her seat and is irritating her horse with an unsteady lower leg and hands: poor horse.

lower leg, since the horse's back is relieved from the weight of the riders seat. This means that the rider's seat bones exert little or no pressure through the saddle. When lateral aids need to given, the appropriate stirrup needs to be weighted accordingly. In the case of half-halts, both ankles need to be weighted downwards and the calves become firmer against the horse. The upper body becomes more upright. The aids through the hands and thus the reins differentiate from dressage only in that in turns, the outside rein should predominate.

This is how it shouldn't look. The rider is behind the horse's movement and is holding onto the reins. As a result the horse is jumping with a stiff back.

The aids for turning when in a forward position.

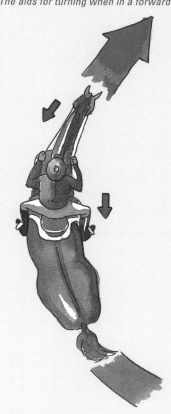

Elbows that stick out, the upper body leaning forwards and to the side of the horse's neck (as if to see whether the horse is really going over the jump), a seat that is too heavy, a lower leg or hands that are not quiet or steady not only look bad but also affect the horse. He may lose his balance, not use his back properly over the jump and – unsurprisingly – this can lead to refusals.

The aids in the forward position

The aids when riding in a forward position are in effect the same as when riding in a dressage position. The aids related to the seat, that is the weight aids, are given more through the knee and

Your position over the jump

When jumping, the rider needs to have a balanced position. You need to be able to move and go with the horse before, over and after the jump. The fence should be approached with a light seat in an even but not too slow pace, heading for the middle of the fence. The rider should look beyond the fence!

During the take-off the rider should smoothly follow the movement. Your hands should go towards the horse's mouth, so that the horse has the greatest possible freedom to use his neck as a counter-balance. The contact to the horse's mouth should not be thrown away! Your seat should float above the saddle, with your upper body bent more forwards. The horse's back should be totally relieved of all weight so it can curve over the jump. Your knees and lower leg should not move!

During the landing your upper body resumes its upright position, the angle with the hip becoming less acute. Your lower leg should not move and your hands should remain quietly to the right and left of the neck. Only when riding on, away from the jump, will the collecting aids again be used, in that your lower leg is used more strongly and your upper body will become more upright. In other words, you will be giving one or, if necessary, more half-halts, while at the same time looking for the next jump.

When taking off, the rider's upper body leans forward...

And upon landing straightens up again.

Here the horse got too close to the jump before take off. He uses his neck as a counter-balance in order to get over the jump without knocking a rail.

Basic exercises over poles

Having practised your forward position in trot and canter sufficiently to ensure a degree of confidence, you can now begin to set out three or four poles in a straight row on the ground. This applies both for walk and trot.

> Tip
>
> There should never be more than five poles in a grid.

Instead of using individual jump poles, it is preferable to use cavalletti set at their lowest height. Set the poles out with a distance of 80 centimetres between each one down the long side of the school. There needs to be enough room before and after the grid so that you can approach and ride on in a straight line. It is a good idea to mark the middle of each pole with a wide piece of tape; this teaches you from the start to aim for the centre.

In a free walk, approach and go over the cavalletti. You should sit quietly and concentrate on your position, which is at this stage unchanged. How much do you need to move your hands so that your horse can stretch down and forwards? Is your lower leg steady and is it strong enough to ensure your horse continues in

a straight line and can't go crooked? How much do you need to apply your leg so that your horse moves forward without hurrying or slowing down?

When everything is to your satisfaction, the cavalletti can be moved to the correct distances for trot. In trot, the distance between poles is between 1.2 and 1.5 metres – the exact distance varies according to the individual horse's stride. In order to quickly measure this distance (you won't always have a tape handy), it is a good idea to measure how long your foot is. Then you will always know how many foot lengths are required to set the right distance. Two poles set at right angles on either side of the first cavalletti will help to ensure that the approach is straight and will prevent your horse swerving away from the poles at the last minute. In the course of the exercise these side poles can be drawn in narrower, until they form a narrow alleyway of 1.5 metres. This will help to make you ride accurately. Later you can do away with this alleyway altogether.

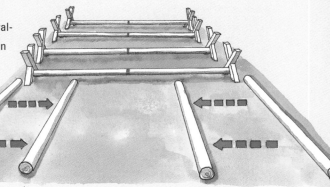

Two poles laid on the ground will help horse and rider make a straight approach to the cavalletti.

1.50 m

When starting out, you may hold onto your horse's mane so as not to jag her mouth. Gradually your hands will need to let go and moved forwards towards the horse's mouth. The inside hand may lightly touch the horse's neck.

Here the reins are knotted and the rider crosses her arms in front of her.

First of all the cavalletti should be ridden in rising trot. Just before the first pole, you should lean slightly forward and hold onto the mane with one hand. Next time, one hand should be moved towards the horse's mouth and soon both hands should do the same until you feel confident. This exercise will serve to take away any concerns and strengthen your confidence.

The second exercise should improve your position through the knees. Now, instead of a rising trot, you should go into a forward position. You should stand in the stirrups with your seat clear of the saddle. You may want to hold onto the mane at first, until you have learnt to use your knees and lower leg to hold and balance yourself independent of the horse's movement.

After you have learnt to stand balanced in the stirrups and adapt smoothly to the horse's movement, comes the hardest exercise. Knot the reins and trot through the grid with your arms crossed in front of you. When you can do this well you will have reached an important milestone: you will be in total balance and will have fully independent hands. This means that you are able to hold your hands quietly even whilst your body moves up and down with the trot. You should be able to give the horse his required freedom through the neck over the jumps and be able to give half-halts before and after the jump. You can sit in balance without having to hold onto the reins, regardless of what pace the horse is at. In other words, you have mastered the forward seat!

Another exercise involving sitting to the trot over cavalletti will give you the feel of the rhyth-

A sitting trot over cavalletti is something for the experienced rider!

mic swinging movement of the horse's back. However this should only be tried by those who already have a soft and independent seat.

By doing this you will learn what this swinging movement through the back feels like and at the same time learn how to adapt your own movement to it. You will find out that when you become tense, the horse will also tense up. The-

re is then a real danger that the horse will suffer or be injured.

Next, one of the poles should be taken out of the grid and set at the end, at the trot distance of 1.2 – 1.5 metres. Now the grid should have a gap in it for an in-between trot stride. This stride should be in exactly the same rhythm and with the same impulsion as the strides over the poles. The

The trot stride in between the poles demands attention from both horse and rider.

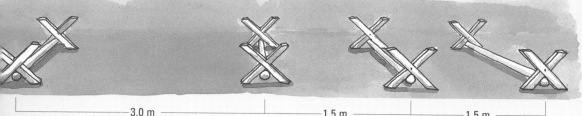

—— 3.0 m ——   —— 1.5 m ——   —— 1.5 m ——

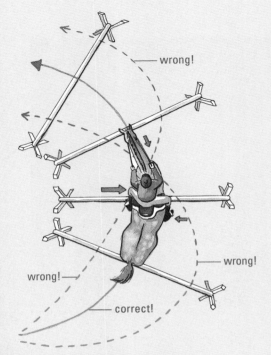

Here the rider has to give very precise aids; this is a demanding exercise! Dotted red lines – Wrong!

it may help to position the poles on a curve or on a full circle. The circle should be ridden as you normally would on the flat, with the horse positioned and bent on the circle. The inner leg drives more whilst the outside leg supports and the outside hand is stronger. In this position the poles are ridden over exactly as if they were in a straight line. This exercise teaches both the horse and rider balance. You can of course also build in a stride without a pole as before.

It is much more interesting and avoids being too repetitive to switch from a grid in walk to one in trot. Build a grid in walk on one half-circle, with another in trot on a different circle. Or combine a row of poles on a circle with one in a straight line that you ride one time in walk and another time in trot. There is no limit to the possibilities. You just need to ensure that you leave enough room between the grids to do other school figures – after all, you don't want to annoy other riders or those who want to use the poles too.

horse also learns to look at what he is doing and the rider learns how to support his horse and ensure an even pace.

Riding over cavalletti on a circle

When a horse "runs" over cavalletti, in other words if he gets faster or rushes through the grid, then

Variations to cavalletti grids

If you need to change a trot grid, then the last cavalletti should always be changed first. If a pole is to be raised, in other words by rolling a cavalletti over to

Frequent changes to the grid will keep the attention of horse and rider.

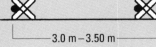

— 3.0 m – 3.50 m —

3.0 m – 3.50 m

position the pole higher, then this should always be done initially to the last in the row. Then the second last, and so on until all the cavalletti have been raised. In walk, the height should not change much so as not to affect the natural rhythm in this pace.

By positioning the poles at differing heights (for example, low, low, high, high or low, high, high, low), the attention of horse and rider will be maintained. Exercises such as this should only be ridden though with a more experienced horse, since the demands placed on a horse when going over cavalletti positioned in the highest position are too much for younger horses.

Canter work

Cantering is the most important pace for riding over both small and large obstacles. A rider must learn how to get her horse on the aids in a forward seat and must be able to shorten and lengthen the canter stride at will. It is best to practise this by lengthening a specific number of

The horse is cantering forwards with plenty of impulsion and ...

... allows itself to be collected without any resistance.

Even at a fast canter, this horse stays securely on the aids.

canter strides before collecting again, either in the school or more ideally in an open area. Imagine that there is a jump in a particular spot, then try and reach this spot in three or four canter strides. When you have no problems in lengthening the horse's frame (the horse's head will go more in front of the vertical) in order to get to the chosen spot, and can then immediately shorten the stride into an almost collected stride, then you can proceed to doing the same exercise over poles.

Working over cavalleti in canter

The goal here is for the horse to canter quietly and rhythmically over the poles. This is why a ground pole is used for young horses or inexperienced riders. If the horse goes over the pole quietly with an almost unaltered canter stride, then the next stage is for a second pole to be laid down 6 to 6.5 metres after the first. The horse should now canter over the first pole, take another canter stride without a pole and then canter over the second pole. If the horse does this calmly and fluidly, then more can be asked for. Three poles should now be laid out at a distance of 3 – 3.5 metres apart, the distance of one canter stride. This means that the horse will canter over a pole at every canter stride, with the fore and hind pair of legs changing over every pole. This arrangement is called an in-and-out or bounce. Gymnastic grids such as this educate the rider's feel for rhythm and are good for the horse. In addition it is a lot of fun to ride grids like this! They should not though be any longer than five poles at most.

As a step up from this, set up a number of small(!) bounces in groups, with one or more canter strides between each set of poles. The horse will go into canter of his own accord over the poles. Since this is a demanding exercise, do it only for short periods at a time and not too often. By positioning the cavalletti at differing heights (always though changing the last one first), the canter grid can be easily altered. Here too, missing out a pole and having a non-jumping will keep both horse and rider's attention.

Mixing straight lines with circles teaches the rider to give clear aids using a lighter seat. The first rule is always to carry out all these exer cises calmly in a smooth and rhythmic canter. If the horse becomes agitated and the rider starts to lose control, then go back a step and do an easier exercise again.

With an in-and-out arrangement, the horse's fore and hind legs change over every pole.

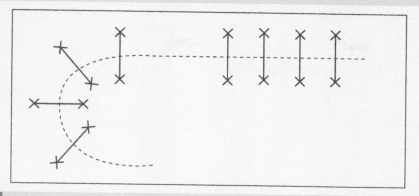

Constantly repeated exercises dull the brain! Let your imagination take over. This is just one example that is easily altered.

Tip

Always approach grids involving bounces at a trot to start with.

Starting to jump

At this stage neither horse nor rider should have any problems riding over cavalletti rhythmically and smoothly at a consistent tempo, even when the grid is altered. You should now have an idea of your horse's ability. You will know when to stop before your horse gets tired or bored. The horse will be securely on the aids and both trot and canter will be well established.

Before putting a rail anywhere near a jump stand though, it is worth summarising the distances used between poles and cavalletti in a grid.

Walk: approximately 80 centimetres, allowing 1.5 metres when there is a stride in between.

Trot: 1.2 to 1.4 metres, allowing 2.5 metres for a non-jumping stride.

Canter: 3 to 3.5 metres, allowing 6 to 6.5 metres for a non-jumping stride.

The height of a ground pole (or placing pole) in a grid is 15 to 20 centimetres, for a cavalletti in its middle position 30 to 35 centimetres and in its highest position 50 centimetres.

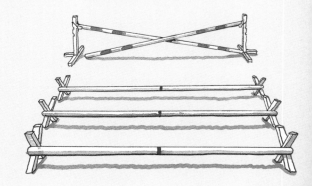

Your first small jump should be a cross-pole.

To start, begin with a row of three trotting poles set at a distance of 1.3 metres. Set a cross pole up 2.5 metres after the third pole using two jump stands so the cross point is 60 to 70 centimetres high.

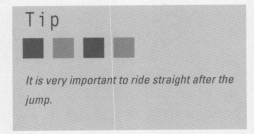

Tip

It is very important to ride straight after the jump.

It is sensible to use cross-poles, as this directs horse and rider to the middle of the jump. The horse should trot as before over the poles and then take off in the middle between the last pole and the small jump, landing in canter.

When he can do this easily, then a second small jump can be added at a distance of 3 to 3.5 metres. Any horse should be able to do a simple bounce from a trot. Don't forget to ride straight after the jump. If your horse gets too excited through the grid, then it is wise to go back to trot and then walk a couple of strides after the jump. This should be repeated until the horse learns to keep calm. The horse needs to wait for your instructions. A grid of three trot poles followed by a bounce can be used in many different ways. One possibility would be to place three small bounces after trot poles followed by a stride and then a small cross-pole. Alternatively, spread the fences further apart (6 to 6.5 metres) to allow a non-jumping canter stride in between. Alternate between ground poles and raised cavalletti (low-high-low-high), or use a small upright as well as cross-poles. The last jump in a grid could even be a small oxer, though these must be approached in canter.

The level of difficulty should now slowly be increased from week to week, but starting with an easy exercise every time you train.

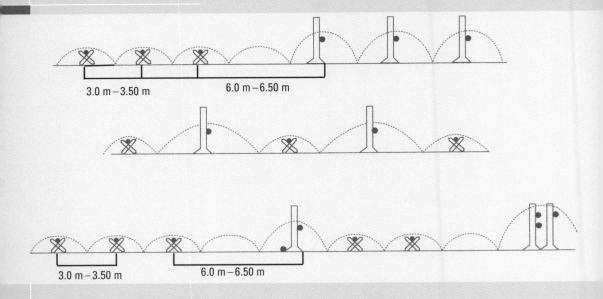

3.0 m – 3.50 m   6.0 m – 6.50 m

3.0 m – 3.50 m   6.0 m – 6.50 m

Airy jumps like this can be difficult for horse and rider to correctly judge take-off.

A placing pole in front of a jump can help get the right stride into the jump.

Tip

Only once you are working comfortably at your current level should you increase the level of difficulty.

When increasing either the height or spread, leave the jumps otherwise unchanged. Only once all is running smoothly should additions, such as fillers, be made to the jumps without changing the height. Alternatively change rustic rails for coloured ones. At this stage it is a good idea to always use a solid ground line, even for the smallest of jumps. If there is no ground line, as when for example a pole is positioned in cups 60–80 centimetres high, then place a pole on the ground as well. Best of all, place two parallel poles one over another and then another at the base of the jump at the foot of the jump stands. Horses can see and judge the take-off to jumps with a ground line, or a densely built jump, much better. Rails that are suspended high up (so-called "airy" or "gappy" jumps) are considerably more dangerous. Jumps like this can do serious harm to young and inexperienced horses and to riders. They can misjudge the take-off, hit the rails, possibly even getting them between their legs, and before you know it there has been a serous accident. It is worth the effort to use a couple of extra poles.

Jumping single fences

For beginners (horse and rider) it's easier to jump through varied grids than a single jump. In addition it gives you useful practice for judging distances and combinations when riding full courses later. To make it easier for a rider or young horse who is still learning to judge their take-off at fences, it is wise to use a placing pole placed approximately 3.5 metres in front of the jump. This can be a cavalletti laid flat, or a pole. This will encourage the horse to take off from a canter stride, for which he needs 3 to 3.5 metres. For the unpractised rider it is fairly hard to judge from a distance how many strides are needed before take-off. If there is a ground pole it makes this task much easier. This will teach the rider to judge whether to ride the approach strongly, or instead to collect the horse up before the jump. It's purely a matter of practice.

In the case of individual jumps there is a greater danger that the horse will approach on a wavering line or crooked angle, and as a result not jump in the middle of obstacle. You need to have the horse securely between your leg and hand. To assist this it is a good idea to use two poles set at right-angles

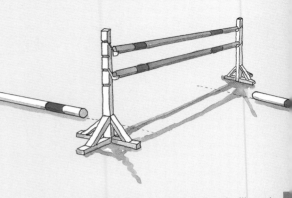

Two poles placed like this on the ground will teach both horse and rider to approach the jump in a straight line and ride away from it straight.

to the jump to contain the horse in the approach. Later you can use one pole placed in front and the other after the jump at right-angles on opposite sides to guide on each side. They should be positioned some way from the jump so that the horse can't jump onto them.

Tip

Don't practise over jumps set at their highest position. This doesn't make any sense at all.

Guide poles on either side will prevent the horse running out the side.

It is important that the horse approaches and is ridden away from the jump in a smooth and rhythmic canter. The height of the jump is then largely irrelevant.

What you need to know to jump a small course

Now you are ready to tackle a small course. When jumping in competition there are certain rules that you need to follow. Besides obviously having to ride in a forward position and using the correct aids, it is also important to walk the course and note at what distances the jumps are placed. Riders are always given time to walk the course before the class begins. You should use this time to walk the course as if riding it. The main things to consider are: how do I fit the required number of strides in so I can approach the next jump in the middle? Where will I need to change rein (i.e. the canter lead)? Where is the start and finish? You should find a plan of the course hung up near the start. Study this carefully, as when you are out on the course it will all look different. When you are finally on your horse at the start of the course it is much better to be relaxed because you know what you are doing.

What is a distance and what is a combination?

A related distance is when a specific number of strides link two fences. Longer distances may be five to six canter strides, shorter ones can be three to four. The rider must either ride the horse on with longer strides or collect the horse so that it canters with shorter strides. The jumps are individually numbered, meaning that if there is a refusal, only that particular fence need be jumped again.

When walking the course you need to carefully consider how you are going to ride it later.

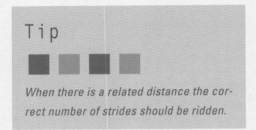

Tip

When there is a related distance the correct number of strides should be ridden.

A combination will consist of a number of jumps that may be built differently (for example, cross-rail, post and rail, oxer). There are different types of combinations – open, closed, part open and part closed. The individual parts of the fence will be numbered the same but with a, b, c added (for example 6a, 6b, 6c). In a combination ridden in canter, in novice classes the distance will be set from 6.5 metres (one canter stride) to 12 metres. For more advanced classes, the distances will be set at 10 to 12 metres at the most, for two canter strides. The rider needs therefore – according to the stride of her horse

– to be able to quickly lengthen or shorten the stride. If a horse refuses in a combination (this usually happens because the rider hasn't ridden on strongly enough), the entire fence needs to be tackled again.

Closed combinations are much harder as you can't get out of the combination because either a hedge, wall or rails blocks the way. There is no option but to get over the refused jump with only one or two canter strides. One of the most famous closed combinations is the Devil's Dyke at Hickstead, used for the Hickstead Derby.

With a partially closed combination there is a way out somewhere on the side within the fences, for example either between the first and second fence or the second and third. When there is a refusal within the closed part of the combination you will have to act as above – you don't have any choice! However, if the refusal happens in the open part of the fence then the whole combination needs to be jumped again.

A closed combination like the Devil's Dyke

The different types of jump

There are four different types of jump:

1. Uprights, such as post and rails, wall, gate.

2. Spreads, such as oxer, triple bar or staircase, fence and ditch and so on.

Water jump

Post and rails

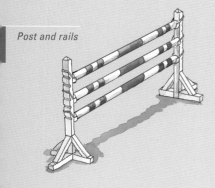

Cross-poles

Triple bar or staircase

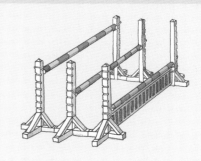

Wall

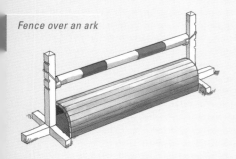

Oxer

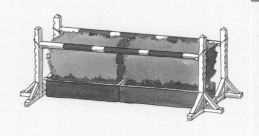

Fence over an ark

25

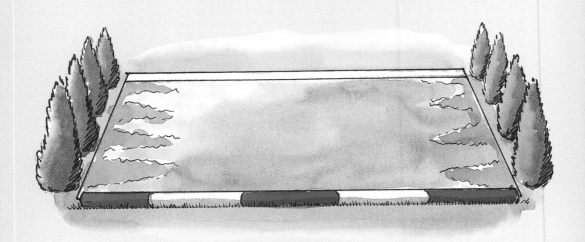

Water jump

3. On and off jumps, such as banks, table tops etc.
4. Water jumps, where no obstacle is placed before, in the middle or after the jump. One small fence of at most 50 centimetres high is allowed at take-off.

What do the flags signify?

Every fence has one red and one white flag positioned to either side. The start and finish lines are also marked in the same way and in both cases the red flag should always be to the rider's right and the white flag to the left when she passes through them. When there are two flags crossed over in front of the jump, then this means that the fence is not part of the course.

When does the bell ring?

The bell (or similar) rings to indicate that the course is ready to be jumped and that the rider may start her round. The rider must wait for this sign; if you start before the bell you will be eliminated. If the bell sounds during a round you should stop. The bell may also be rung if, on refusing or in a fall, the jump is disturbed or knocke down. Once everything is set back in order the bell will sound again; it is imperative to wait for this sign as during the wait the time will be stopped. The second tone starts the clock again. If the bell is rung several times in a row this means that the rider is eliminated, which will be due to something that is wrong with the round – either the horse refused three times, jumped the wrong fence, a fence was completely left out or it took longer than 60 seconds to go through the start flags. If the horse is disobedient for more than 60 seconds at any one time then this also can lead to elimination.

Ring etiquette

In the warm-up area the horse should be ridden enough to be warmed up for the round, but not so much as to make him tired. During the warm-up, jump no more than three or four practice fences.

Tip

What a horse or rider can't perform before a competition won't be learned during the warm-up.

Enter the ring either in canter or at a brisk trot and halt neatly in front of the judges before saluting. You should be facing the judges; remember that this is the first impression you make on them. Saluting over your shoulder as you try and control your horse while he continues to jog along creates a bad impression! By saluting, you are not only greeting the judges but also indicating that you are submitting to their opinions and final judgement.

A good example of a proper salute.

Your first round

The following describes a type of beginners' jumping class popular in Germany, known as 'Stil-springen'. The German word 'Stil' means style, or way of doing something, so this class is judged not only on whether the fences are jumped clear, but also on the way the horse jumps and the rider's style and position and is similar to equitation in thr UK. This typ of class is an excellent way for beginners to start competing in show jumping as it concentrates the pair on the how, and not just the how high or how fast.

These introductory classes have prescribed courses, like a dressage test, so they can be practised at home. The tests usually have a set distance in trot as well as a set canter distance, with a prescribed number of canter strides to be ridden between two points. There is also sometimes a combination in the course. The six to seven (indoor) and seven to eight (outdoor) fences are 0.8 to 1 metre high, and the oxer spread is never more than 1.3 metres wide. Riders may find it useful in their training to construct a course similar to this on which to practice over, to improve their control and technique when jumping.

When tackling the course, after the rider has entered the ring and saluted to the judges, she waits for the bell to ring, signalling that she can start her round. It is essential to wait for the bell, otherwise you will be eliminated before you start. So, don't just take off out of over-excitement! After the bell has sounded trot on (in our example at least). Most tests will actually start in canter, in which case make sure that you canter on so that you go over the start in canter and

While the horse is jumping the fence you should already be looking for the next jump.

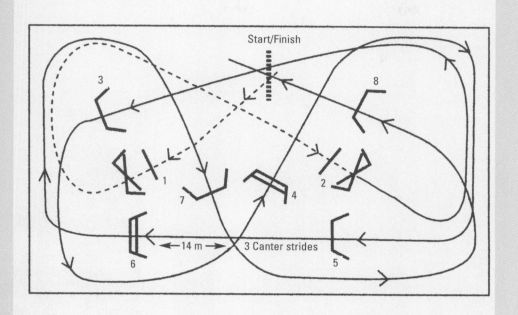

An example of a beginners' show jumping class judged on style.
The dotted line shows where trot should be ridden.

choose the canter lead that you will need for the first jump. In our example the test starts in rising trot. The first jump is a cross-pole (80 centimetres high) with a ground pole placed about 2.5 metres in front of the fence. This should be approached in a straight line in rising trot (don't forget to look at the jump) and then jumped.

Ride away from the jump in a straight line, again in trot and make a wide turn to the right to the second fence. This is also a cross-pole with ground pole, after which you should canter on taking up a forward position. Ride on in a straight line and then make a sweeping left-hand turn to number 3. If the horse lands on the right canter lead after the second jump, go back

to trot and canter on again on the left leg. This transition needs to be done correctly (without pulling or hauling on your horse's mouth) and the horse must accept the aids. In the middle of the long side, turn away from the track and ride on to jump 3. Be prepared as this is an upright without placing pole. Afterwards ride on straight and turn on the left hand in canter until just before the middle of the next long side. You should already be looking at the next jump. One to two horse lengths away from the middle of the long side, turn to the fourth jump, a small oxer. Afterwards try to land on the correct lead (otherwise go back to trot and canter on again) and make a turn to the right to jumps 5 and 6

The rider is sitting in perfect balance over the jump. She allows the horse to stretch out without altering her contact. A perfect example of good jumping style.

(a small upright and an oxer). They are set at a distance of 14 metres, requiring a prescribed three canter strides. This means that if you have a long striding horse you will need to shorten it and if you have a short striding horse you will need to lengthen his stride.

It is important though that you get the first jump right. If the approach to the first jump is short or long then it is going to be difficult to get the correct number of strides between them correct, or you could end up knocking a rail down. Before and between the jumps you need to control your horse so that he can find the right take-off point. This means riding actively forward between the jumps. Although this applies to every jump, it especially applies when there is a pre-set distance or a combination. After fence 6 ride in a straight line on the right hand evenly and rhythmically (which isn't always as easy, after a combination or related distance, as it sounds) in a curve around fence 3 to the seventh fence (again an upright without placing pole). After this ride on the left rein (if necessary going back to trot first) ride back to the track and then into the corner and then in a curve around to fence 8 before cantering on rhythmically through the finish. You must ride between the finish flags, otherwise you will be eliminated.

Please don't forget to ride on through the finish, even if your concentration lapses out of sheer relief in getting round.

How is a style class judged?

Great emphasis is placed on the position of the rider, and especially a correct forward position. The effectiveness of the rider is also important. The entire round should be ridden in an even tempo with the horse always taking off in the right place. Has the rider kept to the right number of strides in the related distance? Any shortening or lengthening of stride should be accepted by the horse softly and submissively. In the turns the horse should be clearly ridden from the inside to the outside rein. It makes an even better impression if, on one of the turns, you give with the inside rein to show that the horse is not reliant on the inside rein. All fences should be approached on a straight line and the horse should be ridden quietly and smoothly away after every jump. As a result of all these impressions, a basic mark for the pair's jumping style is awarded.

If a rail is knocked down (a jumping fault) then half a point is deducted from the style mark for every fence knocked down. If there is a refusal, half a point is deducted for the first refusal and one point for the second refusal. If this happens twice at the same jump then two points are deducted. A third refusal unfortunately means elimination. If either the rider or horse falls, then two points are deducted; if both fall together then they are eliminated. For welfare reasons alone this is a good idea! These rules apply to all tests where the judges are awarding their own marks, rather than the class being judged on faults and time alone.

There is also a time limit within which the course must be completed. If this time is exceeded then a deduction of 0.1 point is accrued for every second over the time. You shouldn't worry about this, though, as there is usually plenty of time to complete the course.

Horse and rider are relaxed after a session of schooling over poles. It's also been fun!

Conclusion

Schooling over poles is an indispensable exercise: not just for young horses, but for all horses, regardless of whether they are going to jump or not! Pole work will help to condition all of the horse's muscles, especially those in the back. It also helps to keep horses fresh and alert, as well as being a welcome change for horse and rider. As a rider, you can develop your balance and feel for the movement of your horse and you will learn more about the ability of your horse than you could by flatwork alone. Schooling over poles also demands awareness of both your own and your horse's safety.